The Wisdom
of
Camilla,
The Queen Consort

© Knightsbridge Publishing
2022

The Wisdom
of
Camilla, the Queen Consort

Copyright © Knightsbridge Publishing Group

All rights reserved.
No part of this book may be used or reproduced by any means,
graphic, electronic, or mechanical, including photocopying,
recording, taping or by any information storage retrieval system
without the written permission of the publisher except in the
case of brief quotations embodied in critical
articles and reviews.

business@knightsbridgepublishing.com

ISBN: 978-0-9810511-8-5

The quotations included in this book have been gathered
via copious sources (analog and digital)
and researched for authenticity and accuracy. Some
quotes collected are being presented without
context, and may therefore be imperfectly worded or attributed.
To the subject/authors, contributors and original sources,
our thanks, and where appropriate, our apologies. – The Editor

Printed in the United States of America & United Kingdom

I really need a gin and tonic!

"

The nice thing is I really love people and I am really curious about them.

'When I sit down with my team before an engagement, sometimes they are horrified as I say I don't want to read the biographical brief because I prefer to prise information out of people. It becomes like a game. The stories that come out, I could write a book about.

I had the privilege of hearing incredibly brave women standing up to tell their stories – harrowing stories that reduced many of us listeners to tears. But with each story, the taboo around domestic abuse weakens and the silence that surrounds it is broken, so other sufferers can know that there is hope for them and they are not alone.

far too often,
those living with
abuse do feel
there is no one
to help. i have
learned how vital
it is to spread
the word about
the help that
is available.

THE NICE THING ABOUT DOGS
IS YOU CAN SIT THEM
DOWN, YOU COULD HAVE
A NICE LONG CONVERSATION,
YOU COULD
BE CROSS, YOU COULD BE SAD,
AND THEY
JUST SIT LOOKING AT YOU
WAGGING THEIR TAIL!

"

No one knows
what goes on
behind any front door.

what particularly concerns me is the rise of osteoporosis in young people and its link with eating disorders.

I HAVE OFTEN SAID THAT DOMESTIC VIOLENCE IS CHARACTERISED BY SILENCE OF THE ABUSED, OF THE ABUSER AND OF THOSE WHO DON'T KNOW HOW TO INTERVENE. BUT THE MEDIA HAVE THE ABILITY TO BREAK THIS CORROSIVE SILENCE BRINGING US THE VOICES OF VICTIMS SHATTERING THE TABOO AND RAISING AWARENESS OF WHAT WE CAN ALL DO TO STOP THIS HEINOUS CRIME.

we all know that reading IS AN INVALUABLE life skill. IT IS VITAL FOR children in THEIR EDUCATION and as THEY TAKE THEIR place in THE GROWN-UP WORLD.

"

You can eat sensibly, exercise and stay trim. You don't have to starve yourself and risk damaging your health irrevocably. We need to make young girls aware of this. We need to drive it home.

To actually leave your home and somebody you have probably been with a long time is very brave.

'We were brought up in a very happy family and I can't whinge about my childhood because it was idyllic.

'I'm ashamed to say that I really hated the Internet. I didn't understand it and I thought, 'What's the point of this?'

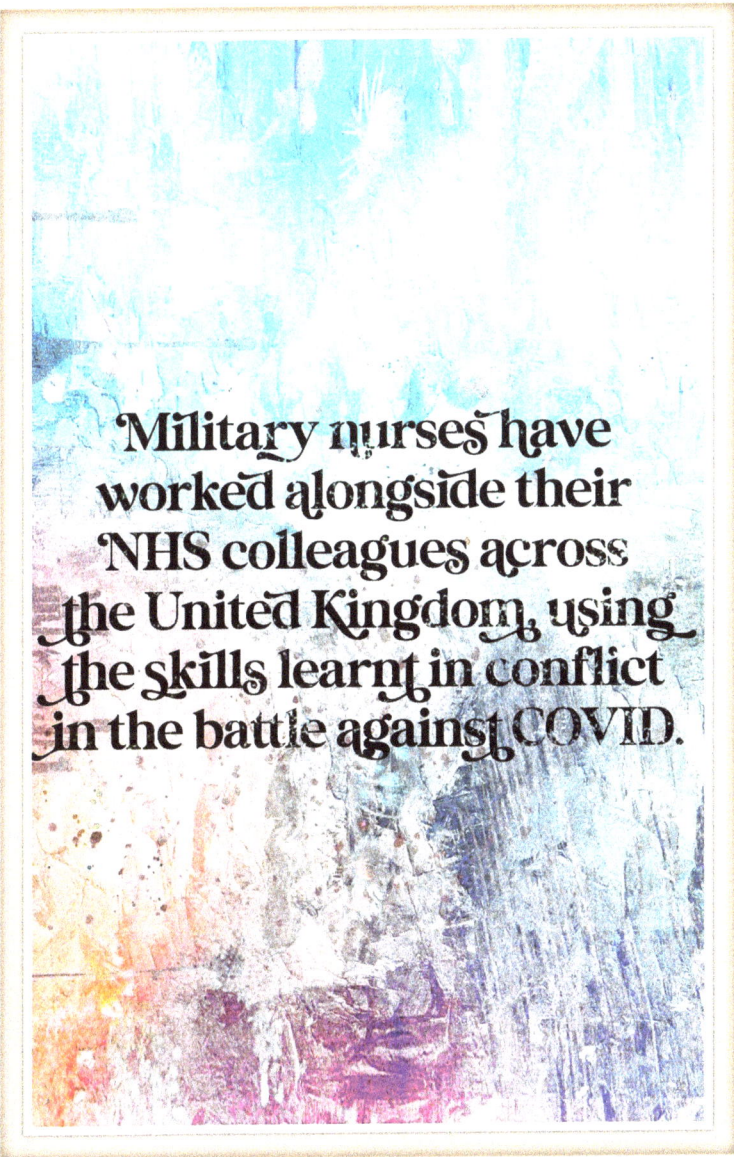

Military nurses have worked alongside their NHS colleagues across the United Kingdom, using the skills learnt in conflict in the battle against COVID.

'I'd be out in my garden all day, every day if I were allowed.

'I don't think I'm tough…but I do think I'm quite a strong character.

"

Sadly, there are many
children who have not
yet been given the chance
to discover the magic of reading,
or set foot in the worlds you
can discover on bookshelves.

If you are a
positive person,
you can do so
much more.

I was very lucky to have a father who read to us when we were children. And he didn't just read books – he brought them alive. We couldn't wait for the next chapter. So my love of reading started early and has stayed with me all my life.

"

The Duke of Edinburgh's philosophy was clear: 'Look up and look out, say less, do more – and get on with the job' – and that is just what I intend to do.

"

Both [The Duke] and Her Majesty have always been the very touchstone of what it truly means to 'get on with the job', and an inspiration to each one of us here to do the same, whatever our age.

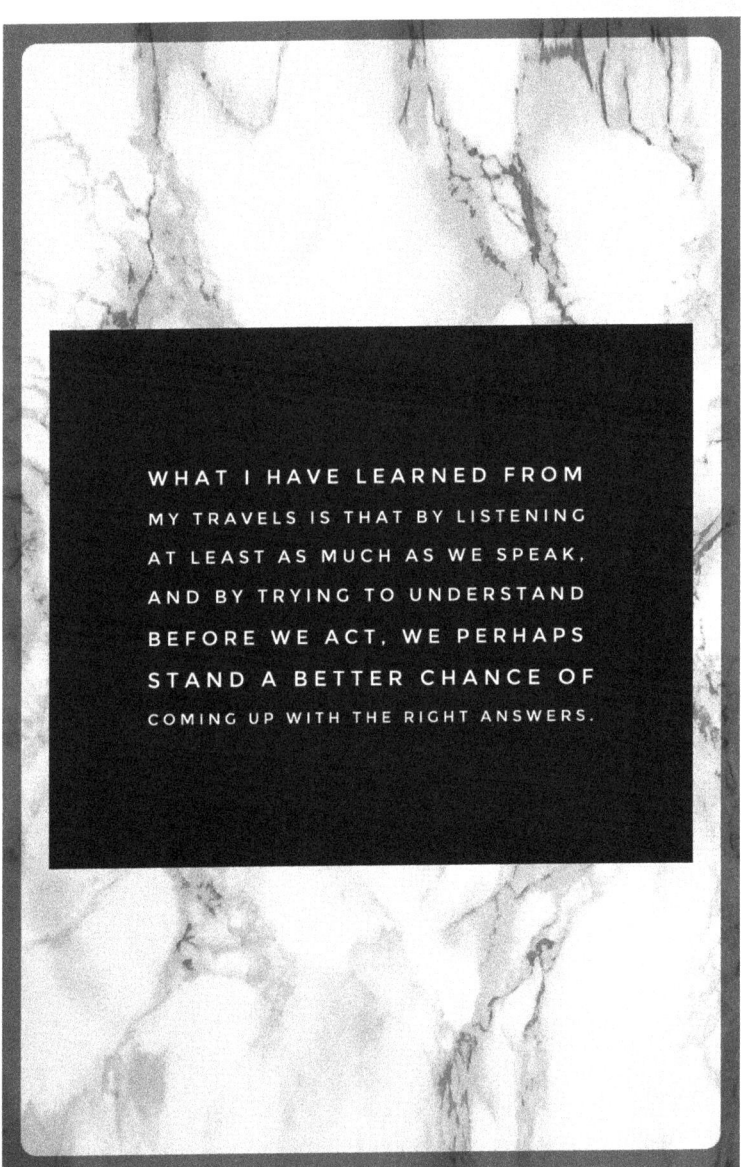

WHAT I HAVE LEARNED FROM MY TRAVELS IS THAT BY LISTENING AT LEAST AS MUCH AS WE SPEAK, AND BY TRYING TO UNDERSTAND BEFORE WE ACT, WE PERHAPS STAND A BETTER CHANCE OF COMING UP WITH THE RIGHT ANSWERS.

MY GRANDFATHER...DECLARED
that 'A woman who cannot
MAKE SOUP SHOULD NOT BE
allowed to marry'.
YOU MIGHT NOT AGREE WITH HIS
rants, but there was no
DOUBTING HIS PASSION FOR PROPER FOOD.

BEING A FRIENDLY
NEIGHBOUR HAS
ALWAYS BEEN THE
KEYSTONE OF
COMMUNITY LIFE
AND JUST SAYING 'HELLO'
CAN SOMETIMES
MAKE A HUGE DIFFERENCE.

> OH, IT'S QUITE ALL RIGHT,
> WE CRUSE QUITE A LOT
> AROUND HERE.

"

You've got to laugh through most things, and sometimes I do laugh a bit too much. There are situations where it's very difficult not to lose it completely, especially, you know, if something goes terribly wrong and everybody sits there for a split second [not sure how to react]. You do have to swallow and pinch yourself very hard to not laugh.

"

...that was always how we were brought up: never complain and never explain. Don't whinge - just get on with it.

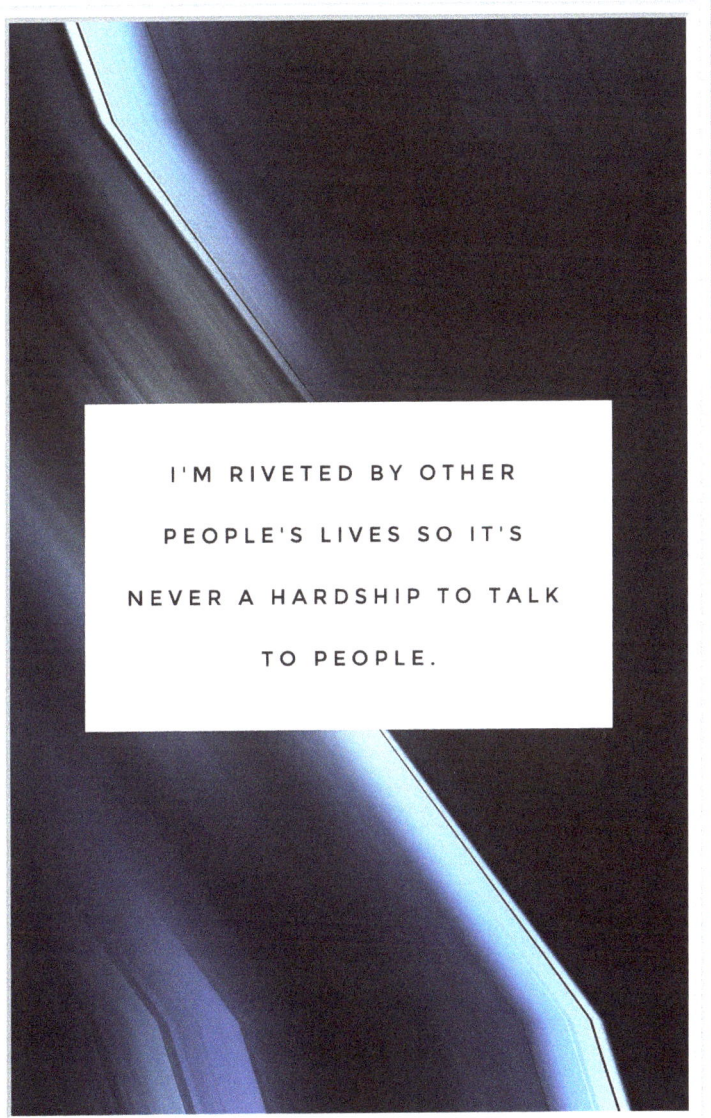

I'M RIVETED BY OTHER PEOPLE'S LIVES SO IT'S NEVER A HARDSHIP TO TALK TO PEOPLE.

Poetry is like time travel, and poems take us to the heart of the matter.

"
My husband is
not one for chilling.

"
Luckily [my husband] has caught up with me now. We are both pensioners and he can join in with me collecting the bus pass.

> MANCHESTER IS A PAST MASTER AT BRINGING LIGHT TO DARK TIMES.

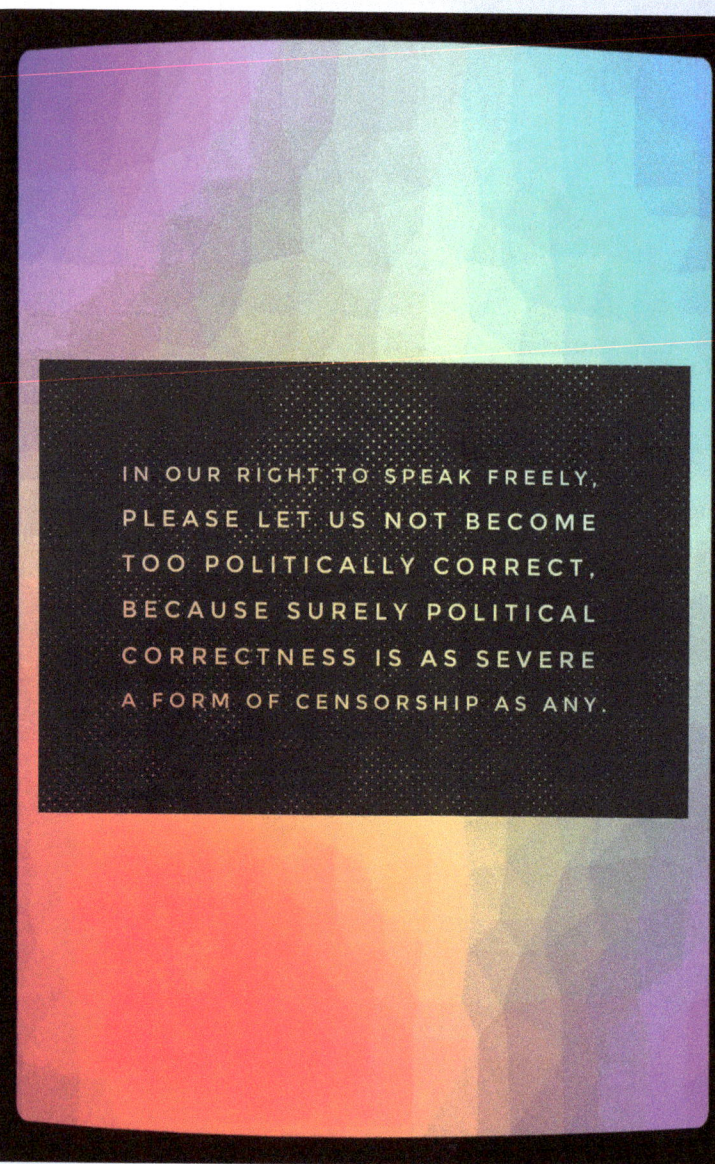

"

I am hopping up and down and saying, "Darling, do you think we could have a bit of, you know, peace and quiet, enjoy ourselves together?"
But he always has to finish something.

IN A WORLD WHERE SO MANY THINGS HAVE CHANGED FOR THE BETTER, THERE ARE — SADLY — STILL MANY VULNERABLE, FORGOTTEN AND NEGLECTED CHILDREN. EACH ONE OF THEM HAS A UNIQUE STORY.

People haven't really acknowledged the issues of coercive control, which can be terrifying, it really is one person's word against another.

Knightsbridge
Publishing
Group

© Knightsbridge Publishing
2022

CPSIA information can be obtained
at www.ICGtesting.com
Printed in the USA
BVHW020834241022
650134BV00022B/628